Passing Thoughts of a Young Old Soul

Orajen Christy

BookLeaf Publishing

Presentation by *BookLeaf Publishing*

Web: www.bookleafpub.com

E-mail: info@bookleafpub.com

ISBN: 9789357745161

First edition 2024

To my mom, my sister, my friends

To my communities,

*To the people who bless me with their presence
and make me believe in myself.*

ACKNOWLEDGEMENT

I'd like to acknowledge BookLeaf Publishing for putting out this challenge. I don't know where this will take me but I'm thankful to have participated and learned more about myself through this process. I'd also like to add a special acknowledgment to the Shakespeare Group at San Quentin for inspiring me to continue with this project.

PREFACE

I decided to participate in the #thewriteangle challenge because I kept seeing it and I had always been writing since I was young. This was a chance to share. It's good practice as a young artist. Thank you for taking the time to read this description.

If you want to know more about my process, during the time of this challenge, I realized what I wanted to do with my life. My life purpose felt affirmed after volunteering at Marin Shakespeare Company at their callbacks. It was my first time being in a professional theatre space setting and I felt like I belonged. I think behind some of these poems are just what came into my head when I was not trying too hard and not trying to make it sound "good". These really are the passing thoughts equivalent to a free write. For part two, during the time of editing the book, I went through a big transition of transferring to University. I had to process through much grief and loss and the idea of moving on and forging ahead to create my own path and the life that I want for myself.

Part One:

The being

Some days

Some days
I don't want
To open my eyes
Get out of my bed
Some days
I can't wait
To return to
Home to my bed
To close my eyes
And begin again

Every morning I wake up
I prepare my mask
soften here
harden there
checking for signs
my natural wear and tear
as well as
stress I buried
that has crept its way
to my surface.

2

Self

I can't pretend to be someone else
I can emulate them with an open mind
I am authentic and genuine
in my attempt to be a better me
I am happy
because I am sad
I am energized
because I have agency
I am strong
because I am weak

I am

Come and Go

The train used to come every winter
When the leaves turned yellow
And drop onto the gravel
Then the train goes come new year
I can't wait for your return
Until I can be the one
That goes to you

Those days

I remember
you had to leave
I cope
you being away
I grieve
Our temporary
Happiness

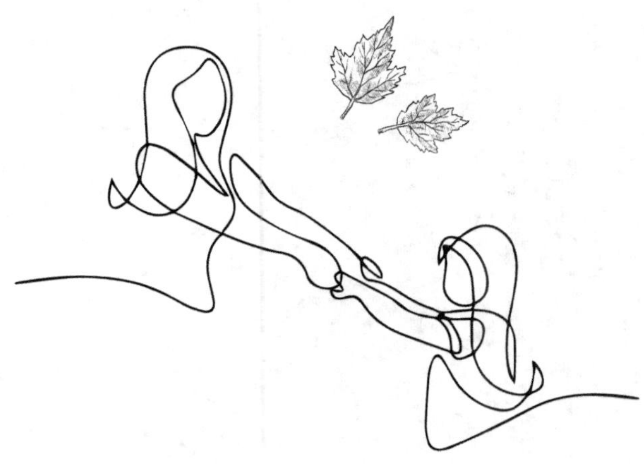

Give and Take

I never knew
How much
I gave
Until I couldn't
Give anymore
I was the taker
From myself
To give to others
I give to myself
Finding those
Who are more
Than
Give or take

Enough

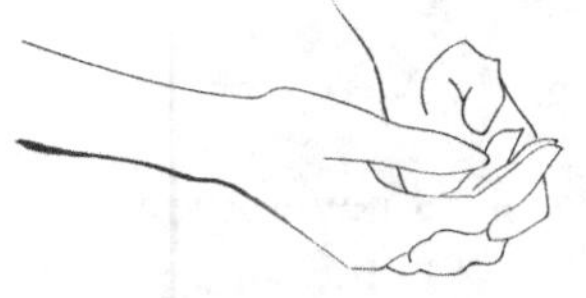

I think of you
sometimes
I was just a child
still a child
you left
on a one way
never to return
but your ghost lives
you haunt me
This mind
This body
my prison
why

someday
I'll stop asking
say goodbye

My Path of Roses

To what degree
of darkness
of sadness

Do I need
to experience
to survive
must I know
the light
the joy

to what degree
must I suffer
to be
able to live
to thrive

to flourish?

Disconnect

Crippled by the weight of
my world
I created
Unable to
bridge the gap
Between my world
And the world
around me
Speak words
Into life
They become
The path
The bridge
I will get
The best
Of both worlds

Roots

I have all
I need but
I still want
More
To push myself
be challenged
To give back

My foundation
is strong
built up by
Love who
Spoil me
Support me
They make me
See what there is
to love so I can love
The confidence to
Live and grow
together
While we have
Each other

Frenemy

It drags me along
Never bending
to my will
But always
Giving me
What I need

Time

Who is that?

12

They is my pronoun
She is my pronoun
One morning
I woke up
And cried
Validated
I dreamt
He is my pronoun
They
She
He
Are me

I remove myself
from the list
of those who
hurt me
abused me
used me
I choose for myself
free
forgiven
I choose to be me
unapologetically

My Disclaimer, My Motive

Tomorrow

I've always found the happy in my sad
I've held on when I wanted to let go
Investing in myself
it becomes joy
from within

energy
not created
not lost
transformed
we are magic.

A familiar stranger

Reflected back at me
I can't recognize
The one who
keeps me
pushes forward
past comfort
past discomfort
I keep growing
with strong roots
bearing fruit

Lifelong Grief

Death
hangs around
on my shoulder
whispering sweet
relief and comfort
it will be over soon
but not
by my own hand

Our eyes to behold

Take
from me
What
you will
of my art
You are
you
I am
me.
May it
resonate
transcend
the lines
the boxes
society
forces
upon us
to conform
together
may we
grow.

one day

one day
it could all change
and
it is okay
be grounded
take it
at your pace
lay down
crawl, roll
walk
when
you're ready you'll know
having
balance
confidence
to run,
to jump
or
keep walking
stroll
strut
march
catwalk

we keep on
we hold on to ourselves

Part Two:

The growing with healing

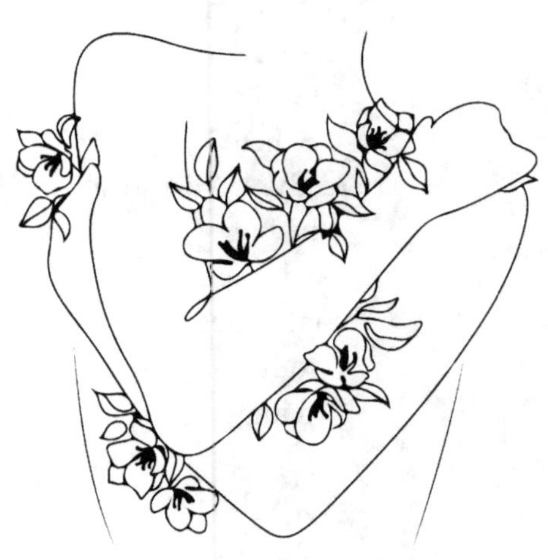

Everything can change in an instant. Thank you
for holding on this whole time. This is the
moment we've been waiting for and working on.

Remember to breathe.
Ground yourself until you find a nice quiet place
to cry. Let it out. Don't keep it in anymore.

Get to know these feelings of discomfort,
frustration, and disappointment. They will let
you know the joy, pride, and accomplishment
even better.

Forgive yourself and be kind.
Let's take care of each other.
You are my baby, my number one.
I'm sorry I'm twenty years late but I'm here now
and I'm not going anywhere anymore.

So give us a chance to be magic.

Say it with me:
"I am articulate and intellectual.
I am deep as well as wide.
I am as beautiful as my mind.
I am firm yet warm and kind."

Doing it for the plot

Before I was so sick and tired of being sick and
tired, but I realize that I did it to myself.
Self-sabotage as a form of false control.

I knew what would happen. I had to.

I'm not used to this new life.
But it is my second chance at having the childhood
I couldn't with the guidance of the one who had to
grow up quickly in me.

Tired redefined:
To reclaim the life I thought I couldn't have
To ask questions
To take opportunities that present to me
To say no or I don't like that

I'm tired and I like it
I'm just getting started

Reflection to my first

Coming up on what would have been our 10 year anniversary, remembering the plans we made and the future we were going to build...

If we had a child, would anything have changed, would I still have left?
I'm sorry I left when I did but it was better than waiting to try to find a good time.
There is never a good time for that conversation.
I had to. If you still resent me, I don't blame you, but I hope you are happy now. Pleased to have moved on and forgotten me.
I didn't know what I wanted then.
I didn't know myself that well while I was trying to survive.

Thank you for loving me during our time together and I'm sorry I couldn't love you more.

Dad[d](y) issues

Don't you know it's your fault?

You didn't give me a Y.

So you can't ask anyone else why,

Not my mother...

Not me...

Why is it that you do not have a son

It is your failure

But you choose to blame us

I'm left to keep asking why

But you had to go off and die

I keep looking for answers that I'll never be able

to find...

Hopefully one day, you'll be out of my mind...

There is no enemy

We navigate life the best we can
Shipwreck of any kind is inevitable
But we hesitate to hold up even a white rag to
surrender
We are but dandelions in the raging winds

Always trying to deny what is
What is not
What being who
She
She is not the enemy

History claims they owe it all to man
They owe it all to the father
Success to the one who sows the seed
Failure to the fault of the mother should the
fruit end up spoiled or bad.
Always getting the blame and never any credit

She just wants to survive too

To live somehow until she finds a chance to
thrive
For her children at the very least
She is not the enemy
Albeit sometimes misguided
Based on what she knows
And has done to survive

We're all left asking why
We fight each other—why?
Because we don't have a Y

y= mx +b
Man = woman being a mother + boy
His favorite formula, society's core value

She is of the same capacity as him
She can be loud, bold and or daring without it
being on a whim
But forced to be in your world and also carry
it…
Conforming the beat of her drum, the sound
of her heart to his?

I can't imagine having to do that
Having to marry, only to carry it all alone with
no support
I'll do the leaving before the leaving is done to
me
I'm not the enemy.
I'm not your son.

I am a sun.
Not the one you wanted,
But a bright and shiny one.
I am the sun who shines brighter than if I were
the son you forced onto me.
Be careful of flying too close to me.

I owe you nothing as you happened to donate
one thing.
I owe it all to my mother.
I owe it all to my sister.
My dual origin.
Orajen Christy.

I am not your M or F.
I am X.

More than the binary
Unlimited by constructs
Breaking free

Signed,
XX

Epilogue to the Future:

Dandelion dreams

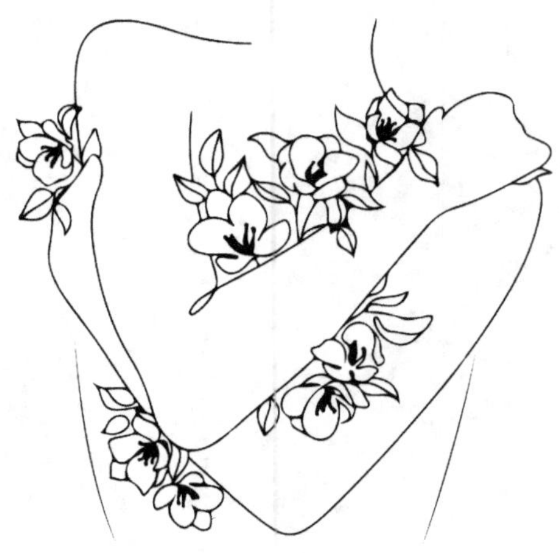

If you hear me speak my word, I am inviting you in as I come out. How someone treats others is more times than not, not personal; but a reflection of their past and present troubles and traumas.

No one can know another 100%
Every one will be the only one
The only original version to be born into the
world.
Timeless originals that cannot be replaced,
never fully replicated.
Stories are shared.
Connections are made.
Words eventually die and are forgotten,
Feelings never die.
This moment we share
Between you and I
Though temporary, it is precious.
Thank you for this gift.
Thank you for seeing me.
Thank you for hearing me.
I can't wait for you to get out and bless this
world. They won't be ready. You will. And if
you need some help, take my hand and let's go.

Dear current me
Dear younger me
Dear future me,

Hi, it's me. I wanted to let you know it's safe
now. It's okay.

In this body.
In this home.
In this space.

Love,
An orchid child